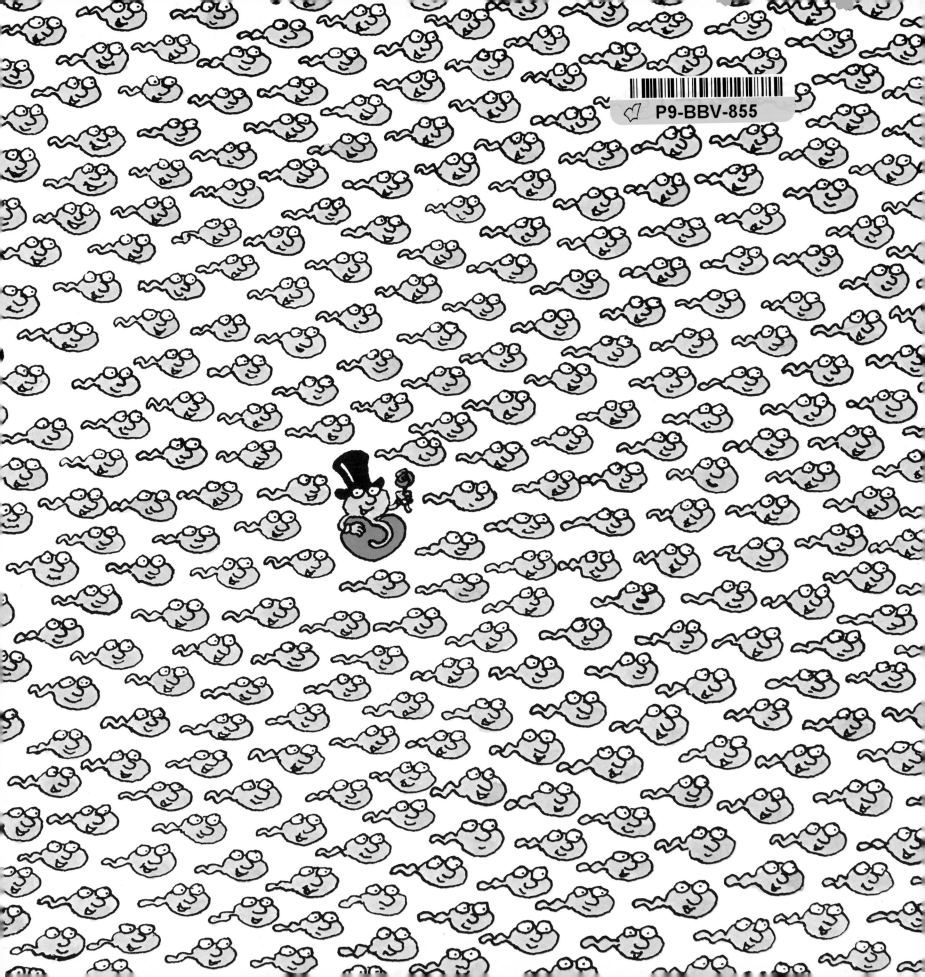
P9-BBV-855

WHERE DID I COME FROM?

"WHERE DID I COME FROM?"

The facts of life without any nonsense and with illustrations.

Written by Peter Mayle.
Illustrated by Arthur Robins. Designed by Paul Walter.

For Simon, Nicholas, Christopher, Jane,
and red-faced parents everywhere.

First published June 1973.
Second printing October 1973.

Copyright © 1973 by Peter Mayle
Library of Congress Card No. 73-78033
ISBN 0-8184-0161-3

All rights reserved. No part of this book may be reproduced in any
form without permission in writing from Lyle Stuart Inc. except
by a newspaper or magazine reviewer who wishes to quote brief
passages in connection with a review.

Typesetting by Conway Group Graphics Ltd., London.
Mechanicals by Ronchetti & Day, London.

Manufactured in the United States of America

Published by
Lyle Stuart Inc.
120 Enterprise Avenue
Secaucus, New Jersey 07094.

This book is all about you.

We wrote it because we thought you'd like to know exactly where you came from, and how it all happened.

And we know (because we have children of our own) how difficult it is to tell the truth without getting red in the face and mumbling.

Anyway, before we wrote all this down, we asked some boys and girls your age where they thought they had come from.

It's difficult not to get red in the face.

Here's what some of them said:

"I was brought special delivery by the stork."

"The cat brought me in one night."

Now, you know that none of that is true.
The truth is much more interesting than that. So
we'll start at the very beginning.

<u>Little people are made by bigger people.</u>
The first thing to know is that babies are made
by grownups. One of them has to be a woman,
and one a man. In other words, the two people
who made you were your mother and your father.

Now, if you put your mother and your
father in the bath together, you'd notice something
interesting.

They are not made at all the same way.
You've probably noticed that already, but you
notice it much more when you put them in the
bath together.

Quite apart from being different sizes,
they are different shapes. And they have different
parts to their bodies.

What the differences are.

This is important, because it's the different parts that make it possible for your mother and your father to make you.

In fact, it's so important that we've done two big pictures so that you can see just what's what.

Don't worry if the pictures don't look too much like your mother and father. The important parts are the same on all of us. (Even you.)

Let's start at the top of the pictures and see what the differences are.

First of all, you'll see that the man has a flat chest. But the woman has two round bumps on her chest.

These bumps have a lot of names. Some people call them the bosom (which you say like this: boozum). Other people call them titties, or boobs. (Don't ask us why.)

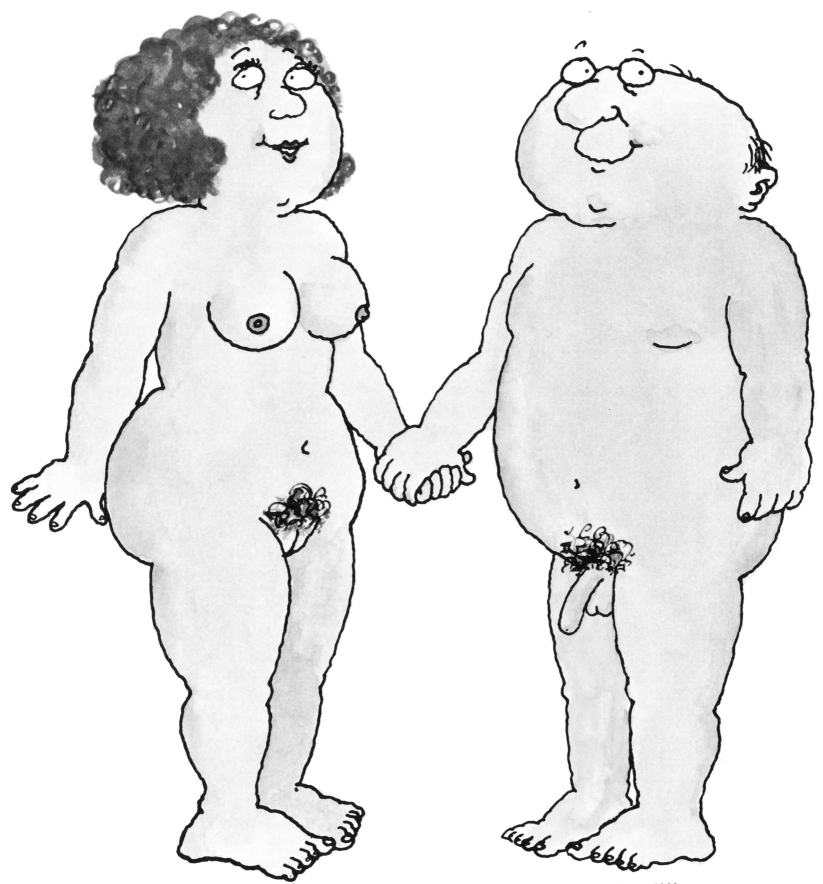

When people take their clothes off, you can really see the differences.

<u>Breasts.</u>
But the proper name for them is breasts, and that's the name we want you to remember.

When you were just born, your mother's breasts were rather like a mobile milk bar. For the first few months of your life, the only food you could eat was milk. (Because at that time, you didn't have any teeth; so you couldn't eat hot dogs or hamburgers or french fries or candy or anything. You had to drink your food.)

Well, the milk that kept you alive for those first few months either came from a bottle,

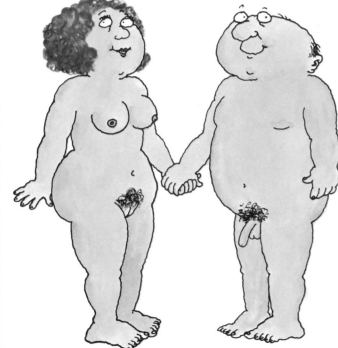

or your mother's breasts. So it's a quick thank you to breasts before we move on.

Take a look further down the pictures. You'll see that just below the middle, the woman spreads out, but the man doesn't.

Aaah. Milk, wonderful milk.

<u>Hips.</u>
The reason she spreads out there (that part is called the hips) is to make enough room for a baby. But that comes later.

Look further down, between the legs. Both the man and the woman have a lot of furry hair there. (Don't worry. You'll have some too as you get older.)

<u>Penis.</u>
But the important thing to notice is that the man has something hanging between his legs that the woman doesn't have. All you boys have one.
And yours will grow bigger as you grow bigge

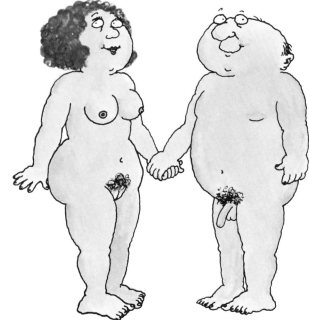

Just like breasts, this hanging part has a lot of different names, too. But the right name for it is penis. Although it's spelled penis, you say pee-nus. (Like peanuts without the 't'.)

So that's what the man has.

It gets bigger as you get bigger.

<u>Vagina.</u>
But what does the woman have between her legs? She has a little opening called a vagina (it rhymes with Carolina).

All right. Now, if you can remember those two names, the penis and the vagina, we'll get on to how a baby is made.

<u>The beginning of a baby.</u>
What happens is this. Let's say the man and the woman are lying in bed together. (This part often happens in bed, because a bed is so nice and comfortable.)

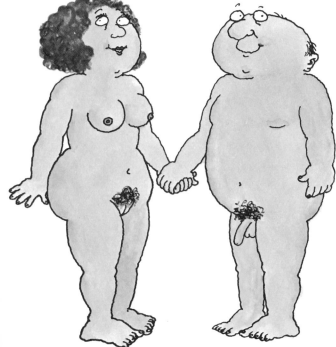

The man loves the woman. So he gives her a kiss. And she gives him a kiss. And they hug each other very tight. And after a while, the man's penis becomes stiff and hard, and much bigger than it usually is. It gets bigger because it has lots of work to do.

New babies start here.

By this time, the man wants to get as close to the woman as he can, because he's feeling very loving to her. And to get really close the best thing he can do is lie on top of her and put his penis inside her, into her vagina.

This is the closest two people can get.

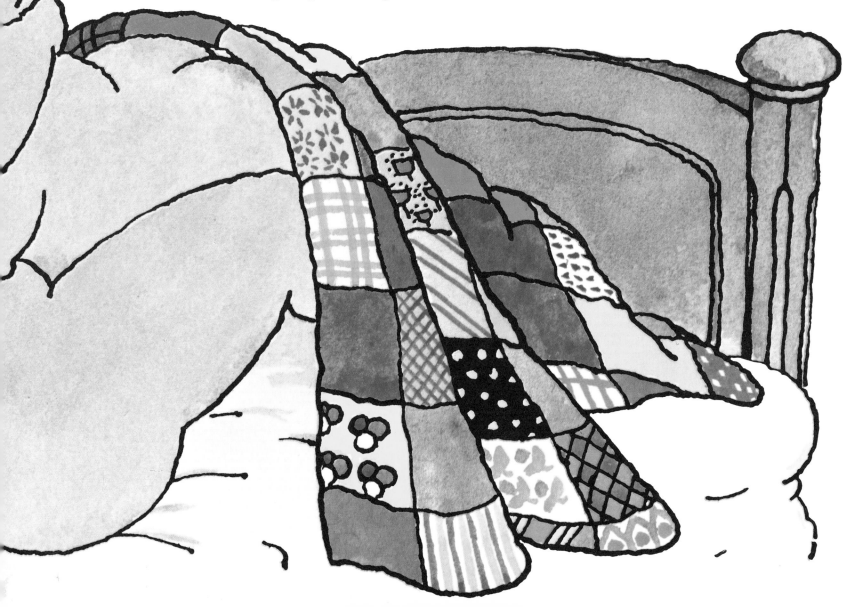

<u>Making love.</u>
This is a very nice feeling for both the man and the woman. He likes being inside her, and she likes him being inside her. It's called making love, because it all starts with the man and the woman loving each other.

It's a difficult feeling to describe, but if you can imagine a gentle tingly sort of tickle that starts in your stomach and spreads all over, that will give you some idea of what it's like.

And as you know, when you're feeling tickly you wriggle about a bit. It's just the same here, except it's a special kind of wriggling.

It's easier to understand when you realize that the parts that tickle most are the man's penis and the woman's vagina. So most of the wriggling happens down there.

It feels a bit like this, but much better.

Well, believe it or not, this sticky stuff is how you and I and all of us started.

It's called semen, and in the semen are sperm.

The romantic sperm.

Each drop of sperm is actually made up of hundreds and thousands of smaller drops of sperm, which you could only see under a very powerful microscope. And what they get up to is quite amazing.

After leaving the man's penis, the sperm make their way up the woman's vagina, like tiny tadpoles swimming up a stream. What they're hoping to find is one of the eggs that the woman produces inside her every month.

Sperm: they're just like tiny tadpoles.

How could an egg resist a sperm like this?

If one single sperm meets one single egg, they have a romance of their own. This is called fertilization, and the result of it is the beginning of a baby. (If two sperm meet two eggs, the result is twins. Three sperm and three eggs, triplets. And so on.)

The sperm and the egg combine to make a tiny person. It's so small that not even the mother knows it's there for a few weeks.

One sperm plus one egg make one baby.

Two sperm plus two eggs make two babies.

And so on.

<u>From a speck to a baby in nine months.</u>
But very, very slowly, it grows inside the mother. It (we should really give it a name, but we're not sure if it's a boy or a girl yet) gets its food from the food the mother eats. It stays safe and warm in a place inside the mother called the womb. (Which you say like this: "woom.")

And over a period of nine months, the speck changes from almost nothing into a full-fledged baby, all ready to come into the world.

You might like to know what happens during those nine months, so we've done a month-by-month chart to show you how an unborn baby grows.

Long before you were born,
you started moving around.

First month.
The baby (let's say it's a girl) spends her first month growing from a dot you can hardly see into a little girl measuring about the size of one of your teeth. As small as she is, she already has a backbone and the first beginnings of arms, legs, nose and eyes. She even has a heart that's beating.

Second month.
By the time the second month has passed, our baby not only has arms and legs. She has fingers, toes, elbows, and knees. And a definite little face.

Third month.
This is the time when the baby starts to develop her shouting equipment. She begins to form her vocal chords, which she's going to need when she starts yelling for dinner.

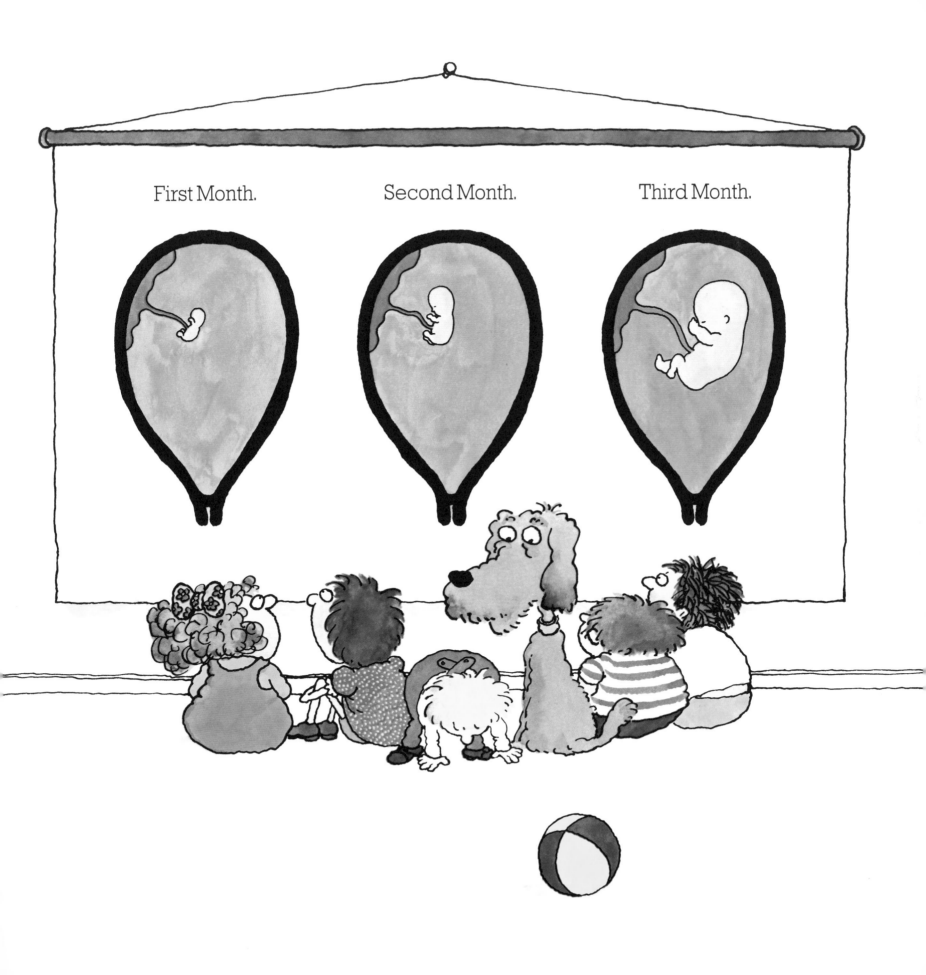

<u>Seventh month.</u>
If you thought she was big before, by now she's a whopper. About as long as your arm (but all curled up), and weighing about three pounds. Now that her body's grown a bit, her brain is beginning to grow too.

<u>Eighth and ninth months.</u>
This time is spent getting bigger and stronger and getting ready to see what the world looks like.

Seventh Month. Eighth Month. Ninth Month.

The Birth Day.

Now we come to the day that all of us have been through and none of us remembers. Our real birthday.

There lies the baby, all curled up inside her mother. How does she get out?

The simple answer is, she's pushed out. After about nine months, Mom's had enough. The baby is now ready to come out, and nature starts things moving in the right direction.

A special kind of stomach ache.

The first sign the mother has is a series of stomach aches, coming at regular intervals. At first, these aches (which are called labor pains) come a long way apart. Gradually, they get closer and closer together, and that's when the doctor starts rushing around. Because that means the baby is really ready.

The doctor: mother's little helper.

The Birth Day.

What the mother has to do is push the baby out through the opening between her legs, and what she uses to do the pushing are all the muscles inside her stomach.

The last part is the hardest.
Now when you think how big the baby is, and how small the opening is, you can imagine what hard work it is for the mother. That's why this part of the birth is called being in labor.

It can take a long time, and it's very, very tiring. But in the end, out comes the baby, looking red in the face, cross, and yelling like a spectator at a football game. (You yelled too when you were born, because it's quite a shock coming into the cold after nine months of being warm and snug.)

Coming out into the world
is quite a shock.

One last thing has to be done before everybody can relax. For the entire nine months of her unborn life, the baby has been getting her food through a little tube that is attached to her stomach.

<u>Why you have a belly button.</u>
Now that she's born, and going to start taking food through her mouth, she doesn't need this tube any more. So the doctor snips it off (it doesn't hurt), ties up the end, and makes it all neat. And that's why you've got a belly button, which is all that remains of the tube that once kept you alive.

This long tube has a really long name: the umbilical cord.

That funny looking belly button once kept you alive.

There. Now you know where you came from.

You may think it sounds like a lot of hard work for such a little person. But there's a very good reason why your mother and father went through it all.

And if you want to know what that reason is, just take a look in the mirror.

It was all done for you.

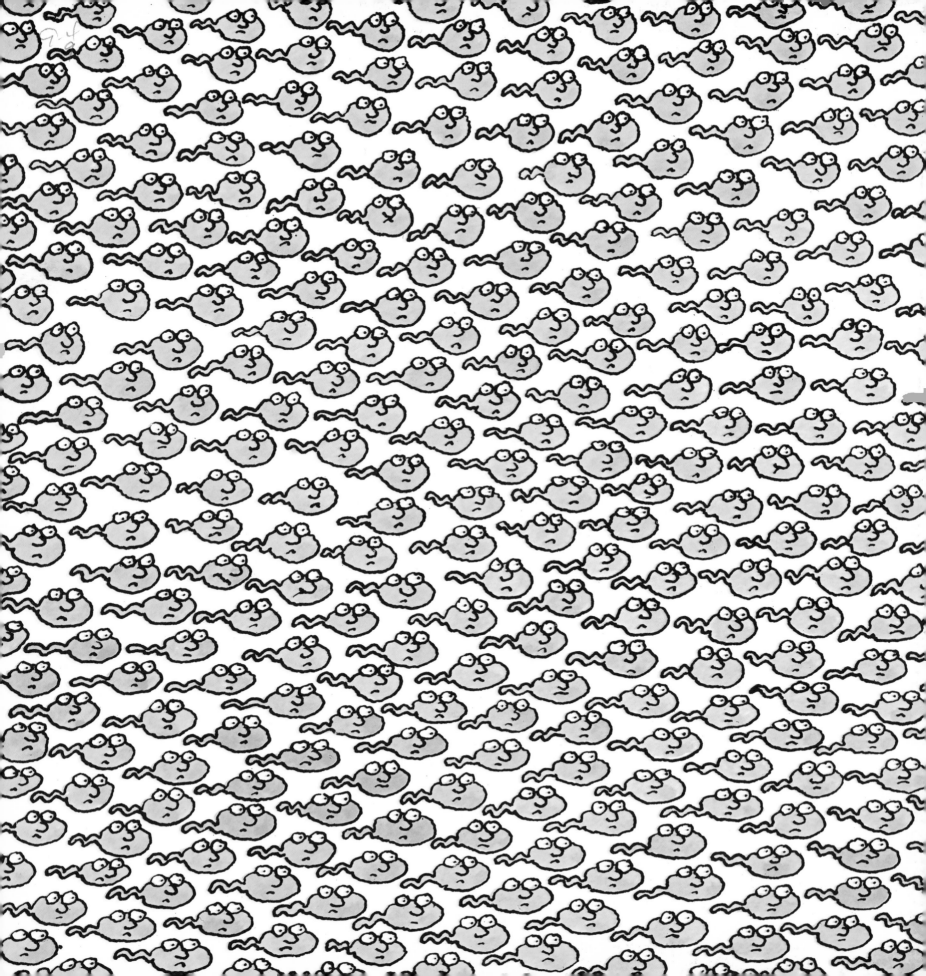